SECOND

JOKES AND RIDDLES

A Humor book for kids 7 years and up

Volume 2

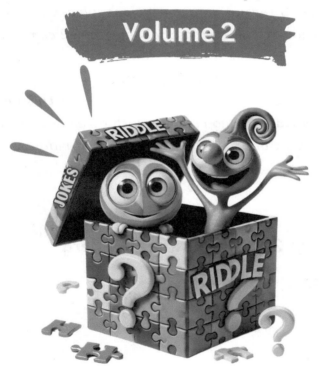

The ultimate playbook for laughter—
packed with the silliest jokes and the
cleverest riddles around!

Contact Information:
For additional information or questions, please contact the author at christianasbookclub@gmail.com.

Acknowledgments:
The author appreciates your engagement with this book and hopes it provides young readers with a fun and engaging introduction to the joy of jokes and riddles.

ISBN: 9798346988267

Table of Contents

How to Explore This Book

Hello, Young Explorers!

Welcome to the amazing world of giggles and brain tickles in "Second Grade Jokes and Riddles, Volume 2"! This book is packed with even more jokes and riddles to make you the star of laughter and the champion of puzzles!

Here's how you can have tons of fun with this book:

Jump Right In: No need to start at the beginning—flip to any page and enjoy a joke or riddle right away! Find the answers after each chapter!

Laugh and Share: Jokes are best when shared, so read them out loud to your buddies, your family, or even during class (with permission, of course!). See who can giggle the longest!

Think and Solve: Challenge your mind with our riddles that make you think outside the book. Guess the answer before peeking at the solution!

Create and Amaze: Got a joke of your own? There's a special place at the back where you can write down your own funny ideas and test them on your friends and family!

Remember, the main rule of this book is to have a blast and share the joy of laughter. Whether you're on a long car ride, hanging out with friends, or relaxing before bed, this book is a great companion to lighten up your day!

Ready to laugh? Turn the page and let the adventure begin!

The Story of Riddles and Jokes

Once upon a time, long before there were books or even written words, people loved to challenge each other's minds and make each other laugh.
This is the story of how riddles and jokes traveled through time and across the world to get to us today.

In the lands of ancient Egypt, around 4,000 years ago, people already enjoyed riddles. Pharaohs and peasants alike would puzzle over tricky questions. One of the oldest riddles ever discovered was found in an Egyptian tomb, written on a stone. It asked, "What is it that has one voice and becomes four-footed, two-footed, and three-footed?" This riddle from the story of the Sphinx challenged anyone who tried to solve it, and it's about the mythical creature that would ask riddles of those who crossed its path.

Fast forward to ancient Rome, where the streets echoed not just with the chariots but with laughter. Romans loved jokes and even had joke books! These were collections of wisecracks that everyone from the senators to the common folk enjoyed.

Meanwhile, over in ancient China, during the times of the great dynasties, riddles were a popular pastime at festivals and family gatherings. They often used word play and were a way to celebrate the beauty of the Chinese language.

As time went on, in medieval Europe, jesters and minstrels traveled from castle to castle. They not only brought news and songs but also carried riddles and jokes from place to place. This was how new laughs and puzzles spread across the lands.

During the Renaissance, a period of great curiosity and learning, riddles became even more popular. Books of riddles were published, showing that people from all walks of life enjoyed sharpening their wits.

In modern times, riddles and jokes have not lost their charm. They have found new life in books, TV shows, and online, continuing to challenge and amuse us just as they did thousands of years ago.

And so, from the deserts of Egypt to your own bookshelf, riddles and jokes have journeyed through history, bringing laughter and light-bulb moments to people of all ages. They remind us that no matter where or when you are from, everyone loves a good laugh and a challenging puzzle!

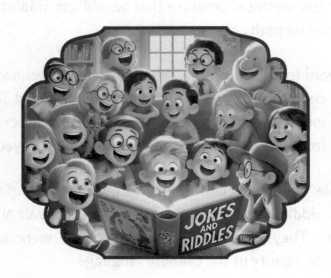

Nature and Environment

Explore the Great Outdoors!

Welcome to the "Nature and Environment" section! Solve riddles and laugh at jokes that bring the mysteries of forests, oceans, and wildlife closer to you.
It's a perfect adventure for young explorers to connect with the natural world.

Riddles

1. What falls from the clouds but never climbs back up?

2. Which tree might you hold with your fingers?

3. I weigh nothing, but you can see me. Put me in a bucket, and I'll make it lighter. What am I?

4. I'm silent but I tell tales, I feed the flames but I'm not wood. What am I?

5. I rush along a path, drink without lips, think without a brain, and rest without sleep. What am I?

Jokes

Why did the tree enroll in school?
To get to the root of all knowledge!

What do you find under wet fur?
A soakin' puppy!

Why do birds fly south in the winter?
It's too long to slide!

What did one autumn leaf say to another just before it fell?
I'm falling for you—catch me in spring!

6. Invisible from sight, I tower beyond the trees, soaring without growth. What am I?

7. I fall from the sky but am not rain, and I'm more beautiful and quieter than hail. What am I?

8. What sort of garment is tailored without fabric and worn publicly without ever touching skin?

9. What type of coat is best dressed on a wall?

10. Which tree is the most cheerful?

Jokes

Why don't oysters share their pearls?
Because they are shellfish!

What kind of plant grows on your hand?
Palm trees!

Why did the flower take a nap?
Because it was bushed!

What do you get if you cross a dog and a daisy?
A collie-flower!

11. What wears a jacket, but shouldn't be eaten?

12. Visible once in a moment, twice in a millennium, but never in a hundred years. What am I?

13. I begin tall and end short, burning brightly in between. What am I?

14. I dance in the winter sky but never fall. What am I?

15. You see me once in June, twice in November, but not at all in May. What am I?

Jokes

Why did the tree visit the dentist?
It had a bad case of root decay!

Why do trees seem suspicious on sunny days?
They just seem a little shady!

What do you call a well-dressed lion?
A dandy lion!

Why are fish so smart?
Because they live in schools!

Brain Bender Boulevard

1. All day I sip on water yet my belly never swells. Guess what I could be that's always thirsty?

2. I stand straight with a spine that holds me up, but I don't have any bones. What could I possibly be?

3. I wear a cool jacket when it's hot outside and switch to warm pants when it's cold. What am I that changes clothes with the seasons?

4. Forever hungry, I need to be fed or I'll fade away, and whatever I touch quickly turns red. Can you guess what I might be?

5. You can catch me easily but throwing me is impossible. I can run very fast, yet I never walk. What do you think I am?

Brain Bender Boulevard

6. As I grow taller, I also grow downward. It's a bit of a puzzle! What could I be that grows in two directions?

7. I'm surrounded by rings, but none of them would fit your fingers. What am I that carries these curious rings?

8. I can travel all around the world, seeing many sights, but I never leave my little corner. What could I be?

9. It's black when you get it, turns red when you use it, and becomes gray when you're done with it. What am I that changes colors like this?

10. Every autumn I fall down gently, but I'm never injured. What am I that tumbles gracefully each year?

Nature and Environment Answers

1. Rain!
2. A palm!
3. A hole!
4. Paper.
5. A river!
6. A mountain!
7. Snow!
8. A lawsuit.
9. A coat of paint!
10. A smiley (pine) tree!
11. A potato!
12. The letter 'M'!
13. A candle.
14. A snowflake!
15. The letter 'E'!

Brain Bender Boulevard

1. A plant!
2. A cactus!
3. A dogwood tree! *(Referring to its bark and leaves)*
4. Fire!
5. Water!
6. A stalactite!
7. A tree!
8. A stamp!
9. Charcoal!
10. Leaves!

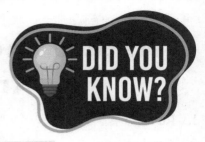
DID YOU KNOW?

Amazon Rainforest:

The Amazon Rainforest produces about 20% of the world's oxygen and is often called the "Lungs of the Earth."

Biodiversity:

Madagascar is home to more than 200,000 species of plants and animals that don't exist anywhere else in the world.

Tallest Tree:

The tallest tree in the world is named Hyperion; a coast redwood in California, it's nearly 380 feet tall—that's taller than a football field is long!

More than 70% of our planet's oxygen is produced by the ocean. The tiny plants in the ocean called phytoplankton do more photosynthesis than the vast forests on land!

Bamboo is one of the fastest-growing plants in the world. Some species can grow up to 35 inches in just one day!

Venus flytraps only close their traps if the tiny hairs on their inner surfaces are touched twice within 20 seconds. This prevents them from wasting energy by closing for false alarms like falling leaves or raindrops.

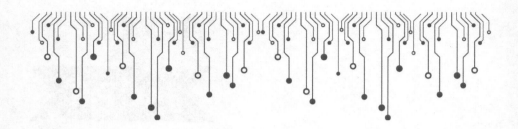

Technology and Inventions

Unlock Innovations!

Dive into "Technology and Inventions," where riddles and jokes spark curiosity about everything from ancient tools to modern gadgets.
Challenge your brain and uncover the fun side of the creations that have transformed our world. Perfect for curious young minds ready to explore and innovate!

1. I have keys but don't lock doors, I ignite dreams but start no fires. What am I that can open worlds with a tap and play without a band?

2. What invention makes walls transparent, letting you see what's hidden behind them without moving a stone?

3. I have many ports but don't set sail, I connect the world but remain in place. What am I that can link many but travel nowhere?

4. I wake you with music but can't be played. What am I that starts your day with a tune, but isn't an instrument?

Jokes

Why did the smartphone go to school?
Because it wanted to improve its "cell" skills!

What do you get when you cross a robot and a tractor?
A trans-farmer!

How do robots eat guacamole?
With computer chips!

Why was the computer cold?
It left its Windows open!

5. I'm not alive, but I stay connected with 5G. What am I that can communicate far and wide?

6. I outline virtual spaces without physical barriers, guarding data with no gates. What am I that encircles information yet never walks the line?

7. What can go up and down without ever moving from its spot, seen on many homes and buildings?

8. I have a ring but no finger to wear it. What am I that alerts with a sound, often heard but not worn?

Jokes

Why did the computer go to the doctor?
It had a virus!

How do you stop a robot from destroying you and the rest of civilization?
You don't press its buttons!

What did the digital clock say to the grandfather clock?
Time's up, old timer!

Why was the robot angry?
Because it had too many wires crossed and needed a reboot!

9. I crave energy without end, starve if unplugged, and devour apps with each byte. What am I that lives by the charge and dies with the drain?

10. I speak without a mouth and hear without ears. I have nobody, but I come alive with wind. What am I?

11. I follow you all the time and copy your every move, but you can't touch me or catch me. What am I?

Jokes

Why did the computer keep sneezing?
It had a "bug"!

What do you call a computer floating in the ocean?
A Dell rolling in the deep!

What makes a computer so smart?
It listens to its motherboard!

What did the spider do on the computer?
Made a website!

Riddles

12. What becomes sharper the more it is used, essential for cutting through problems and solutions alike?

13. Full of holes yet capable of holding water, what am I that defies the usual expectations?

14. I have one eye but cannot see a thing. What am I, serving a purpose without a view?

15. I have cities with no buildings, rivers without water, and forests without trees. What am I?

Jokes

Why don't robots have brothers?
Because they all come with "sister" boards!

Why was the computer tired when it got home?
Because it had a hard drive!

What do you get when you cross a computer and a lifeguard?
A screensaver!

What is a computer's favorite snack?
Microchips and salsa!

Brain Bender Boulevard

1. Seen in every digital screen's reflection, yet never affected by the pixels' dance, what am I that observes without changing?

2. It can fill a room with brightness or color, creating scenes without occupying space. What invention changes a room without a physical presence?

3. Whether corded or wireless, I am always ready to capture your words. What device am I that converts sound into signals?

4. Accessible with a touch, I appear under your fingertips but vanish when you try to catch me. What am I that exists in cyberspace but not in hand?

5. Not a creature of dawn but I can wake you with tunes or beeps. What invention am I that starts your day but isn't organic?

Brain Bender Boulevard

6. Always running but never tiring, I manage your day without moving. What device am I that keeps time but has no feet?

7. I'm riddled with pathways for electrons, holding vast information despite my physical breaches. What am I that stores knowledge digitally?

8. Present globally and resting in your hand, I connect you to the world. What am I that embodies technology's reach?

9. It sharpens each time it is used, solving puzzles and storing answers. What part of technology am I that enhances with activity?

10. I feature in cameras and robots, possessing an eye yet blind to the view. What part of modern gadgets am I that captures but doesn't see?

Technology and Inventions Answers

1. A computer keyboard.
2. A window!
3. A router or a hub.
4. An alarm clock!
5. A smartphone!
6. A firewall.
7. Stairs.
8. A telephone!
9. A smartphone.
10. AI voice assistant.
11. A digital footprint.
12. Your brain! *(Highlighting the invention of puzzles and mental exercises.)*
13. A sponge! *(An early human invention for holding liquids.)*
14. A needle! *(A tool essential in the invention of clothing.)*
15. A map! *(An essential invention for exploration and technology.)*

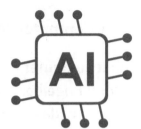

Brain Bender Boulevard

1. A shadow.
2. A projector.
3. A microphone.
4. Digital data.
5. An alarm clock.
6. A clock.
7. A circuit board.
8. A smartphone.
9. A computer processor.
10. A sensor.

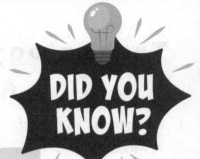

The First Computer Mouse

The first computer mouse was invented by Doug Engelbart in 1964 and it was made out of wood!

The Invention of the Light Bulb

Thomas Edison is often credited with the invention of the light bulb, but he actually wasn't the first to create it. He improved upon previous designs and made the first commercially practical light bulb.

Smartphones

The first smartphone was created by IBM in 1992 and was called "Simon." It had a touchscreen and included applications like an address book, calendar, calculator, and notepad.

The first digital computer was called the ENIAC, which stands for "Electronic Numerical Integrator and Computer." It was completed in 1945 and was so large it filled an entire room, yet it could perform only basic arithmetic!

GPS technology, now common in cars and smartphones, was originally developed in the 1970s by the U.S. military to help soldiers and vehicles navigate accurately anywhere in the world.

The first camera phone was sold in 2000 in Japan. This innovation allowed people to send pictures directly from their phones for the first time, changing the way we communicate and share moments!

Under the Sea

Explore Ocean Wonders!

Plunge into the "Under the Sea" section and discover the hidden world beneath the waves through engaging riddles and playful jokes.
Learn fascinating facts about sea creatures and ocean mysteries. It's an underwater adventure perfect for young explorers keen on marine marvels!

1. I might seem set for a hairdo under the waves, with arms ready to curl and wave. What am I, swaying but not swimming?

2. No royal blood, yet I sport a crown in the deep blue. What am I, reigning over reef without a throne?

3. In ocean's dark depths, I shine my own beacon to charm my next meal. Who am I, dining by the light of myself?

4. Sidestepping along the shore, many-legged but surf-shy. What am I that scuttles but doesn't swim?

Jokes

What do you call a fish that knows how to fix things?
A hammerhead shark!

Why did the fish blush?
Because it saw the ocean's bottom!

What do you get when you cross a fish and an elephant?
Swimming trunks!

What kind of fish plays the guitar?
A bass!

5. Mistaken for flora, I'm a colony of fauna, swaying in currents unseen. What am I, mistaken for a plant?

6. Eight-armed and clever, I escape enclosures but don't juggle books. What am I, a master of marine mazes?

7. Often mistaken for moody, I cling tightly to rocky shores and hulls alike. What clingy sea creature am I?

8. Graceful in my aquatic ballet, but beware my sting if you stray too close. What dancing danger am I?

Jokes

What did the ocean say to the pirate?
Nothing, it just waved!

Why do seagulls fly over the sea?
Because if they flew over the bay, they'd be bagels!

How do you make an octopus laugh?
With ten-tickles (tentacles)!

What do you call a fish that can grant wishes?
A fairy codmother!

9. Home is where the shell is, ever changing as I roam the seabed. What mobile marine am I?

10. Invisible by day, by night I dazzle with an ethereal glow. What luminous spectacle am I?

11. My songs serenade the sea, echoing deep and wide. What large lyricist am I?

12. Though I might seem like I belong in the sky, I swim in the deep sea and use my beak to eat. What might I be?

Jokes

Why are fish so good at watching their weight?
Because they have lots of scales!

What do you call a fish with two knees?
A tunee fish!

What do you call a fish that's a famous detective?
Sherlock Herring!

How do fish get to school?
By octobus!

13. Often called gentle giants, I prefer to move slowly through warm waters, munching on plants. What am I?

14. Capable of diving deeper than any submarine, yet I breathe air and jump above the waves. What am I?

15. I may resemble a treasure chest hidden under the sea, but inside me, you'll find the precious gift of pearls. What am I?

Jokes

Why don't fish do well on school tests?
Because they're always swimming below the "C" level!

What do you call an underwater spy?
James Pond, licensed to swim!

What did the fish say when he hit the wall?
Dam, that hurt!

Why did the fish live at the bottom of the ocean?
To avoid the net-working up top!

Brain Bender Boulevard

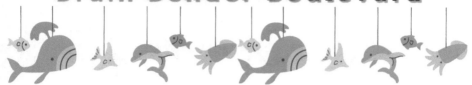

1. I am the silent wanderer of the deep, cloaked in darkness, yet never asleep. With a lantern to guide my way, whom do I light up to catch my prey?

2. Known for my elaborate house that I carry on my back, I change it out as I grow, making a new home from an old foe. What am I?

3. I have no bones but many arms, and if I lose one, it's no alarm. I can regrow it without a farm. What sea creature am I?

4. Though I sound like I might squirt you, I'm known for my inky escape. What am I, with eight arms and a bulbous head?

5. I can dance without legs and sing without a voice. I brighten the ocean with my luminous choice. What am I known for my glowing art?

6. My name might make you think of a bird, but I'm all about scales and fins. Who am I that flies underwater?

7. My garden doesn't grow in soil but spreads vast and colorful under the waves. I'm not a plant, so what am I?

8. I am the king of camouflage, changing my colors and even my shape, hiding in plain sight in the aquatic landscape. What cunning creature could I be?

9. With a mouth that can expand and a body that can inflate, I'm a spiky creature, not one you'd want to agitate. What am I?

10. I build my castle with the smallest grains, crafting spiral towers that remain. Who am I, a craftsman under the tide?

Under the Sea Answers

1. Sea anemone.
2. A starfish.
3. Anglerfish.
4. A crab.
5. Coral reef.
6. An octopus.
7. A barnacle.
8. A jellyfish.
9. A hermit crab.
10. Bioluminescent plankton.
11. A whale.
12. A squid.
13. A manatee.
14. A dolphin.
15. An oyster.

Brain Bender Boulevard

1. Anglerfish.
2. A hermit crab.
3. A starfish.
4. A squid.
5. Bioluminescent jellyfish.
6. A flying fish.
7. A coral reef.
8. An octopus.
9. A pufferfish.
10. A sand dollar.

Immense Pressure

At the deepest point in the ocean, the pressure is more than 8 tons per square inch, equivalent to having about 50 jumbo jets piled on top of you!

The Largest Mountain Range

The Mid-Ocean Ridge is the longest mountain range in the world, stretching about 65,000 kilometers (40,390 miles) underwater, and most of it remains unexplored by humans.

The Ocean's Blue

The ocean is blue because water absorbs colors in the red part of the light spectrum, leaving colors in the blue part visible.

UNDER THE SEA

LEARN
MORE

The Mariana Trench is the deepest part of the world's oceans. Located in the western Pacific Ocean, it reaches a depth of about 36,000 feet (nearly 11 kilometers), which is more than Mount Everest's height above sea level!

The immortal jellyfish (Turritopsis dohrnii) can theoretically live forever. When faced with stress or physical attack, it can revert to its juvenile form and start its life cycle anew, escaping death.

The mimic octopus can imitate up to 15 different marine species, including flounders, lionfish, and sea snakes, not just to hide from predators but sometimes to scare them away. This makes it one of the most incredible adaptors in the ocean!

Bites of Delight

Taste the Fun!

Dive into "Bites of Delight," a flavorful collection of food-themed riddles and jokes designed to tickle your taste buds and challenge your mind.
Enjoy a menu of witty puzzles and sweet surprises, perfect for young food lovers ready to explore the delicious side of fun!

1. I'm a perfect circle on a baker's table, sweet not just by flavor but through a hole in the middle. What am I?

2. Encased in my own natural package, I can be transformed by heat in many ways, yet always begin as a simple shell's secret. What am I?

3. The more you remove, the larger I appear, delightfully sweet as you consume me layer by layer. What am I?

4. Clothed for all seasons and loved for my mash, I'm a staple from the ground. What am I?

JOKES

What does a lemon say when it answers the phone?
Yellow!

What do you call a fake noodle?
An impasta!

What do you call an avocado that's been blessed by the pope?
Holy guacamole!

5. Silent in the choir but loud in a sandwich, I'm often heard in a can. What am I?

6. Striped and sweet, I stand tall with a curve, a favorite treat when winter's at bay. What am I?

7. I shift shades as I mature, and when I'm soft, I'm ready to eat. What mellow fruit am I?

8. Famous for sneaking into milk, I'm sweet alone or with a glass. What am I?

What do you call a sad strawberry?
A blueberry!

What did the grape do when it got stepped on?
It let out a little wine!

What kind of music do coffee beans like?
Brews music!

9. Famed in games for being tossed, I'm hot in the kitchen but cool in the field. What am I?

10. I blush in the field and sweeten your meals, from breakfast bowls to evening treats. What berry am I?

11. Tiny but mighty, I can dress up desserts or sneak into shoes if you're not looking. What am I?

12. I wear a seasonal grin and light up Halloween, from pies to porches. What am I?

Why did the yogurt go to the art exhibit?
It wanted to get a little more cultured!

What did the baby corn say to the mama corn?
"Where's pop corn?"

What do you call an old snowman?
Puddle!

13. Some think I'm nuts, but I'm smooth with chocolate or on your morning toast. What am I?

14. I explode in heat and am a movie's best friend. What snack am I?

15. Hiding under leaves, I'm a tart surprise, perfect for jams or a fresh snack. What am I?

What do you call an apple that's a comedian?
A pun-apple!

What did one strawberry say to the other strawberry?
If you weren't so sweet, we wouldn't be in this jam!

Why did the scarecrow become a successful chef?
Because he knew how to turnip the right eats!

What did the gingerbread man put on his bed?
A cookie sheet!

Brain Bender Boulevard

1. I'm red when I'm ripe and green when I'm young, with a crown on my head, I'm fun to be flung. What am I?

2. I wear a tough jacket outdoors and I'm the favorite of monkeys. Peel back my layers and sweet rewards await. What am I?

3. I'm a green gem in the rough, hide in a brown case, and my heart is guarded by a hairy face. What am I?

4. You might mistake me for a vegetable, but I'm a fruit to the core. I wear a cape of green and bring color to your pizza. What am I?

5. I can be as sour as a puckered face or sweet as a sunny day. I'm hard outside but liquid inside. What am I?

Brain Bender Boulevard

6. Dressed all in purple with a cap too big, I'm small but mighty in your morning fig. What am I?

7. Often in a bunch, I hang around; step on me, and I'll make a sound. What am I?

8. Round and sweet, with a star in my heart, I wear my colors bright but hide in plain sight in many a grocery cart. What am I?

9. You need a ladder to reach my highest bunches, I'm sweet and yellow and perfect in bunches. What am I?

10. I'm small, red, and sweet, with a secret cap that I keep. I'm not a cherry but am often in a fairy tale. What am I?

Bites of Delight
Answers

1. A donut.
2. An egg.
3. A cone of ice cream.
4. A potato.
5. A tuna (tune-a).
6. A candy cane.
7. A banana.
8. A cookie *(as in cookies and milk)*.
9. A hot potato.
10. A strawberry.
11. A blueberry
12. A pumpkin.
13. Peanut butter.
14. Popcorn.
15. A blackberry.

Brain Bender Boulevard

1. A strawberry.
2. A banana.
3. A kiwi.
4. A tomato.
5. A lemon.
6. A blueberry.
7. Grapes.
8. An apple.
9. A mango.
10. A raspberry.

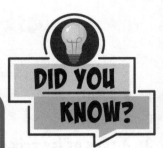

Chocolate was once used as currency

In ancient Mayan and Aztec cultures, cacao beans were so valuable that they were used as currency in trade transactions.

Bananas are Berries, Strawberries Aren't

Botanically speaking, bananas are berries, but strawberries are not. Berries are defined as having seeds inside, and a strawberry's seeds are on the outside.

Apples Float Because They Are 25% Air

Apples can float in water because they are 25% air, which also makes them great for bobbing on Halloween.

The largest fruit in the world is the jackfruit. A single jackfruit can weigh up to 100 pounds and contains dozens of sweet, sticky segments inside.

Honey is the only food that does not spoil. Archaeologists have found pots of honey in ancient Egyptian tombs that are over 3,000 years old and still perfectly edible!

Popcorn has been around for thousands of years; ancient cultures in Peru were popping corn 6,700 years ago. Popcorn became a popular snack in the United States in the mid-1800s, especially at fairs and carnivals.

Time Travel Detectives

Journey Through Time!

Become a "Time Travel Detective" and decode history's mysteries! This section features riddles and puzzles from different eras, perfect for young detectives eager to explore the past in a fun and engaging way.
Gear up for a historical adventure filled with discovery and laughter!

1. Guarding its realm with stone stacked high, where soldiers marched and arrows flew by. What enduring guardian am I?

2. Submerged in silence, lost beneath waves, a mythical city that the sea craves. What rediscovered place am I?

3. Not merely desert mounds but tombs of lore, where pharaohs rest, amid legends of yore. What am I, standing proud and high?

4. A marketplace of old, now still, where columns fall and time does spill. In Greece, I drew crowds from far and wide. What place am I, where shadows now reside?

JOKES

What kind of lighting did Vikings use?
Norse lights!

How do time travelers spice up their food?
With thyme travel!

What do you call a dinosaur that knows a lot of words?
A thesaurus!

5. An ancient circle on windswept plains, where stones stand silent, keeping their claims. What timeless sentinel am I?

6. Tall and steadfast, I cast light far, guiding night wanderers from where they are. What beacon am I, a sailor's delight?

7. A mighty barrier, not just of stone, a fortress long, by an emperor's throne. What am I, stretching far and wide?

8. In an arena of old, where the crowd's cheers grow, I faced fierce beasts and delivered a show. What ancient entertainer am I?

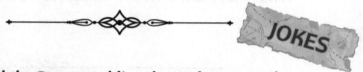

Why did the Roman soldier always lose at cards?
Because he could never deal with defeat!

What dance was very popular in 1776?
The Liberty Waltz!

What do you call a time-traveling train?
The Chrono-Express!

What's a historian's favorite fruit?
Dates, they're always in era!

RIDDLES

9. I carry water across arches of stone, from distant mountains to your home. What Roman invention am I?

10. The heart of Rome, echoing tales of old, where Caesar walked, and stories were told. What historic forum am I?

11. Waters healing, under vaults of stone, where Romans bathed and secrets were known. What ancient spa am I, still famed today?

12. A path laid by legions, for conquest and trade, binding the empire where soldiers paraded. What am I, a road of Roman make?

JOKES

What do you call a caveman's fart?
A blast from the past!

Why do time travelers make great musicians?
They always bring their own "tempo"!

What's a medieval ghost's favorite game?
Hide-and-shriek!

Why did the Sphinx give up on riddles?
It was tired of people giving it the cold "shoulder"!

13. Beside the Nile, I watch and wait, guarding kings with a stony gaze. What vigilant guardian am I?

14. High above, a divine scene plays, lost for ages, now meets the gaze. In a Vatican chapel, where do I reign?

15. Not read for leisure but a guide so vast, charting stars and skies, for sailors cast. What navigational tool am I, from ages past?

JOKES

Why don't ancient secrets ever stay hidden?
Because they belong in a hiss-tory book!

What kind of music did the Pilgrims like?
Plymouth Rock!

How do you make a dinosaur float?
You need two scoops of ice cream, some root beer, and a prehistoric reptile!

Why was the Roman ruler so calm during the storm?
Because he knew after rain comes a reign!

Brain Bender Boulevard

1. I am a place, once lost, now found, where ancient scripts were all around. My discovery brought back a tongue that hadn't been spoken, read, or sung. What am I?

2. Across desert sands, I made my route, carrying silks and spices to boot. Not a single road but a network grand, connecting the East to the Western land. What am I?

3. I'm a structure high and grand, seen in India across the land. Built by a king, so history told, for his queen to remember in fold. What am I?

4. In London's heart I did appear, in a year that brought much fear. A burning flame, from wood to stone, changed the city's skin and bone. What am I?

5. I circle the earth, a line not straight, dividing the dates, I seal your fate. Invisible in the air, yet crucial for when you travel here to there. What am I?

Brain Bender Boulevard

6. I'm a library vast, not of books but of the past. Carved in stone, in Egypt, I last. What am I?

7. My face is a dial, my hands can tell, the movement of the sun, as on earth it dwells. What ancient device am I?

8. Found deep in jungles, covered in vine, my stones tell stories of sun and divine. A lost city, golden and grand, who am I, do you understand?

9. I am a vessel of ancient creed, with a myth about my deed. Lost at sea, yet found again, I carried Greeks to Troy's end. What am I?

10. I stretch across, from sea to sea, once divided lands, now make them free. A marvel of modern engineering feat, connecting waters where two oceans meet. What am I?

Time Travel Detectives Answers

1. A city wall.
2. Atlantis.
3. A pyramid.
4. The Agora.
5. Stonehenge.
6. A lighthouse.
7. The Great Wall of China.
8. A gladiator.
9. An aqueduct.
10. The Roman Forum.
11. Roman baths.
12. A Roman road.
13. The Sphinx.
14. The Sistine Chapel ceiling.
15. A star chart.

Brain Bender Boulevard

1. The Rosetta Stone.
2. The Silk Road.
3. The Taj Mahal.
4. The Great Fire of London.
5. The International Date Line.
6. The Temple of Karnak.
7. A sundial.
8. El Dorado.
9. The ship of Theseus.
10. The Panama Canal.

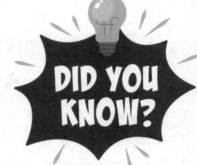

The Enigma Machine

During World War II, the Germans used a cipher machine called the Enigma to send coded messages. It was considered unbreakable until the code was cracked by Allied cryptanalysts at Bletchley Park, which significantly helped to shorten the war.

Secret Writing

The ancient Greeks and Romans used a device called a scytale to send secret messages. A piece of parchment was wrapped around a stick, and the message was written across it. When unwrapped, the message appeared as a jumbled sequence of letters that could only be read by wrapping it around another stick of the exact same diameter.

The concept of time travel isn't just in movies; it's also a serious topic in physics! Albert Einstein's theories suggest that time travel could theoretically happen if you could travel faster than the speed of light.

The Voynich Manuscript is a mysterious book written in an unknown language or code. Dating back to the 15th century, it is filled with illustrations of unknown plants, astronomical diagrams, and odd figures, and to this day, no one has deciphered its contents.

The Ancient Egyptians used to write hidden messages inside the pyramids that weren't discovered until thousands of years later. These messages were often blessings or information about the pharaoh buried inside.

Art and Music

Art and Music Awaits!

Step into a world where art and music blend, with each riddle and puzzle crafted like a masterpiece. This section combines colorful trivia and tuneful challenges, perfect for young creatives ready to explore their artistic side. Ready your imagination for a symphony of colors and sounds!

1. Mounted on slides, I take you on visual journeys through painted scenes and photographed lands. What carousel am I?

2. Whether drawing delicate lines or sweeping across violin strings, I'm never center stage in drama's rings. What versatile tool am I?

3. Ever present yet often overlooked, I hold treasures against gravity's pull. What am I that keeps art aloft?

4. With black and white keys under fingers' dance, I spin melodies that enhance romance. What melodic creator am I?

What's an artist's favorite sport?
Draw-ing!

Why do artists never win at hide and seek?
Because they always draw attention!

What do you call a cow that can play a musical instrument?
A moo-sician!

What's a cat's favorite color?
Purr-ple!

RIDDLES

5. I stretch and hold, silent in my grip, essential in desks but never in a music clip. What am I?

6. Small yet stylish, I add flair to ensembles, often found adorning necks at concerts' crescendos. What am I?

7. My keys unlock melodies, not doors, playing tunes that soar. What musical instrument am I?

8. Combine artistic strokes with boxing blows, what punny name do we bestow?

JOKES

Why did the artist get cold?
Because he ran out of blankets and only had canvas!

What's a skeleton's favorite musical instrument?
The trom-bone!

Why did the artist keep his paintbrush in his pocket?
In case he needed to draw his weapon!

What do you get when you cross a canary and a lawn mower?
Shredded tweet!

RIDDLES

9. Why did the artist end up behind bars?

10. What is a sculptor's favorite kind of dessert, especially when working on statues?

11. Which type of music causes fear in balloons everywhere?

12. I am not just any painting; I cover entire walls or ceilings and tell grand stories through vivid scenes. What am I?

Why did the musician sit on a ladder?
To hit the high notes!

What do you call a painting by a cat?
A claw-stroke masterpiece!

Why do painters always fall for their models?
They find them "picture-perfect"!

What did the sculptor say to his sculpture as he was chiselling it?
"It's chiseled to meet you!"

RIDDLES

13. It's bright orange and sounds just like a tropical bird. What is it, often seen in art classes?

14. What type of artwork is always seen as fresh and moist, no matter when you view it?

15. How come a musician might also be an excellent carpenter?

JOKES

Why did the pianist keep all his money in the bass keys?
Because he liked his cash to be low-key!

Why did the middle C key get invited to all the piano parties?
Because it was in the center of the "action!"

Why didn't the musician worry about playing in the lightning storm?
Because he was a great conductor!

What's a math teacher's favorite type of music?
Algor-rhythms.

Brain Bender Boulevard

1. I'm a grand assembly of black and white keys, each a stepping stone to harmonious melodies. Strike my keys in sequence to unleash magical tunes. What am I?

2. Crafted from wood and strung with care, my voice sings in hands that dare to strum or pluck with rhythm and soul. What am I that makes music whole?

3. Seen on the sides of trains and buildings alike, I am the canvas of the city, where colors play and messages stay. What vibrant art am I?

4. I'm not a musician, yet I play records with a needle, spinning tales in rhythms and beats. What am I, turning tables into musical feats?

5. Composed of dots and lines on staves, I translate silence into symphonies, read by those who understand my script. What am I?

Brain Bender Boulevard

6. Crafted with light and hues, my glassy surface tells stories in colors, glowing in sunlight at sacred sites. What am I that filters light into stories?

7. Tiny and clicked in dance, I bring rhythm to the feet with every clap. What am I, adding Spanish flair to every step?

8. Immovable once set upon the wall, my colors tell tales tall, a permanent mark of artistic gall. What grand visual am I?

9. In artists' hands, I come alive, from broad strokes to fine lines. What am I, a tool that dances with color and design?

10. From a rough block I emerge, shaped by vision and chisel's urge. What transformative art form am I, born from marble or clay's sigh?

Art and Music Answers

1. A carousel *(referring to a slide carousel in art presentations)*.
2. A bow *(for drawing in art and playing on violin)*.
3. A picture hook.
4. A piano.
5. A rubber band.
6. A bow tie.
7. A xylophone.
8. Muhammad Dali.
9. Because he had a sketchy background!
10. Marble cake.
11. Pop music.
12. A mural.
13. A carrot *(often used in still life paintings)*.
14. A watercolor.
15. He knew his scales and could measure in accord.

Brain Bender Boulevard

1. A grand piano.
2. An acoustic guitar.
3. Street art graffiti.
4. A DJ's turntable.
5. Orchestra sheet music.
6. A cathedral's stained glass window..
7. Flamenco castanets.
8. A large-scale wall mural.
9. An artist's detailed paintbrush.
10. A stone sculpture.

The Longest Music Performance

There's a musical performance called "Longplayer" that started on January 1, 2000, and is designed to continue without repetition until the last moment of 2999, lasting for a thousand years. It's being played in real-time from a combination of Tibetan singing bowls at a listening post in London.

The Hidden Mozart

Wolfgang Amadeus Mozart composed a piece that was discovered in his personal catalog but was lost to the world until 2015. This piece, thought to be written in 1773 when Mozart was only 17, was found in a late 18th-century composer's handwritten notebook.

Vincent van Gogh only sold one painting during his lifetime, "The Red Vineyard." Despite his lack of commercial success, today he is one of the most famous and influential figures in the history of Western art.

Leonardo da Vinci designed an instrument called the Viola Organista, which combined the characteristics of a string instrument with those of a keyboard. Da Vinci never built the instrument during his lifetime, but in 2013, a Polish pianist constructed it based on Leonardo's original sketches.

The world's oldest musical instruments are flutes made from bird bone and mammoth ivory, found in a cave in Germany. These flutes are estimated to be over 40,000 years old, showing that music has been a part of human culture for millennia.

Dino Discoveries

Discover Dinosaur Secrets!

Embark on a prehistoric journey with "Dino Discoveries," where you'll solve riddles and puzzles about the magnificent giants of the past. Learn about different dinosaurs, their ancient environments, and the paleontologists who uncover their mysteries.
Dive into an era millions of years ago and unearth the secrets of these incredible creatures!

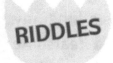

1. Though winged, I soared not through the skies but walked with a beak and stared with ancient eyes. Covered in frills, not feathers, who could I be?

2. Massive as mountains, my footsteps silent as snow, I dined on treetops where no predators could go. What gentle giant am I?

3. Feathered and fierce, I stalked on two legs, not today's avian, but a predator instead. What ancient hunter am I?

4. Armored with a club tail, ready for a fight, I defended myself with more than just might. Who was I, sturdy and strong?

JOKES

What do you call a dinosaur that's always gossiping?
A Gossip-saurus!

What do you call a dinosaur that's always in the game?
A Try-ceratops!

Why can't you hear a pterodactyl go to the bathroom?
Because the "P" is silent!

5. Feared by many, revered as a king, my reign in the Cretaceous was a fearsome thing. Who was I, ruler of the ancient lands?

6. My back was a fortress, and my mouth was a gate, I was as ready for salad as I was for a scrape. What am I?

7. My neck could sweep the treetops, a gentle giant indeed, browsing on foliage, living at a leisurely speed. What long-necked dinosaur was I?

8. Fins for swimming, teeth for dining, I prowled the ancient seas, not flying. What marine hunter was I?

JOKES

What do you call a dinosaur with an extensive vocabulary?
A thesaurus!

What made the Archaeopteryx the best at catching worms?
Being the original early bird!

Why did the Brontosaurus never get invited to sleepovers?
Because he was a notorious Bronto-snorer!

9. Feathered and fleeting, I soared but didn't roar, bridging the gap between dinosaurs and birds. Who am I, a flyer of the Jurassic?

10. Adorned with facial horns and a famous frill, from the Cretaceous period, I'm known for my will. Who am I, with a trio of horns to boast?

11. My arms were short, but my fame is long, a star of the silver screen, fierce and strong. Which iconic dinosaur am I?

12. Where modern games are played, my remains are often displayed. In what ancient remnants might you tread?

JOKES

Why did the T-Rex eat his steak raw?
Because he couldn't find a grill big enough to handle it!

What's it called when a dinosaur has a traffic accident?
A Tyranno-crash-aurus!

Why was the dinosaur ghost avoided at parties?
Because he was a real Scare-dactyl!

13. Known for my speed and lethal toes, I was a terror to those who froze. What swift predator was I, feathered and fierce?

14. From an egg I came, and in herds I thrived, sometimes imagined in your dreams where I survived. What kind of youthful dino was I?

15. Sunbathing with my solar plates, I was a Jurassic creature that no predator baits. Who am I, with my back to the sun?

JOKES

What do dinosaurs use to decorate their kitchen floors?
Jurassic tiles!

What do you call a dinosaur that snores so loud it shakes the jungle?
A Thunder-snoarus!

What do you call a musical dinosaur?
A Rap-tor!

What's explosive and prehistoric?
A DINO-mite display!

1. What ancient creature could see just as well as you and I but never watched TV?

2. I might sound like a magical beast from a fantasy tale, but I'm really a prehistoric fish eater. What dinosaur am I?

3. There existed a dinosaur with an incredible knack for timing. This dino could have been the perfect historian, keeping track of ages and epochs with precision. Which dinosaur could this be?

4. Consider a dinosaur that was not only gigantic and fearsome but also exceptionally smart, mastering numbers better than many creatures of its time. What is the name of this mathematical giant?

5. Imagine a dinosaur that had the capability to connect millions globally like the internet does today, yet it preferred the lush, expansive landscapes of its time to roam freely. What dinosaur might this describe?

6. Picture a dinosaur that carries a crown of horns upon its head, ruling over its territory not by royal decree but through sheer presence. Found in the sediment layers of old, yet absent from any man-made pit. Who could this be?

7. This dinosaur's name might make you think of a doorbell, but it's far more interested in sprinting through the underbrush, chasing down its next meal. What could this speedy creature be?

8. Which dinosaur would you expect to find keeping everything in order, from its nest to its diet? This creature is as neat as they come, never leaving a trace of its meals behind.

9. Among the ancient voices of the past, one dinosaur knew all the tales from the era of giants and beasts. Who could recount such ancient stories with the wisdom of ages?

10. Which dinosaur could boast about having the most extensive network of friends, connecting with herds and packs far and wide across the prehistoric landscapes?

Dino Discoveries Answers

1. A pterosaur.
2. Brachiosaurus.
3. Velociraptor.
4. Ankylosaurus.
5. Tyrannosaurus Rex.
6. Stegosaurus.
7. Diplodocus.
8. Plesiosaur.
9. Archaeopteryx.
10. Triceratops.
11. T-Rex.
12. Dinosaur fossils.
13. Velociraptor
14. A baby dinosaur.
15. Stegosaurus.

Brain Bender Boulevard

1. The Vision-raptor.
2. Plesiosaur.
3. The Chronosaurus.
4. A Mathrodocus.
5. The Connects-you-lot.
6. Triceratops.
7. Veloci-ringer.
8. The Compso-gnathus *(composing neat-thus)*.
9. The Historiopteryx.
10. The Socialsaurus Rex.

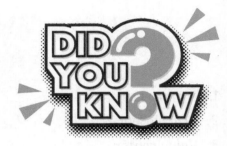

Dinosaur Heartbeat

Some scientists estimate that the huge Sauropod dinosaurs, like the Brachiosaurus, had hearts that weighed as much as 500 pounds and had to pump blood up to their heads, which were sometimes 40 feet above their hearts.

Tiny arms, big fears

The Tyrannosaurus Rex, one of the most famous dinosaurs, had very small arms compared to its huge body. Despite those tiny arms, it was one of the fiercest predators, with a bite force strong enough to crush bone!

The Stegosaurus dinosaur had a brain the size of a walnut – one of the smallest brain-to-body ratios of any known dinosaur. Despite its massive body size, its movements and behaviors were likely very simple due to this tiny brain.

Dinosaurs roamed the Earth for about 165 million years! That's way longer than humans have been around. They lived during a period called the Mesozoic Era, which is divided into three periods: Triassic, Jurassic, and Cretaceous.

Birds are actually considered modern dinosaurs! Scientists believe that many birds evolved from a group of dinosaurs known as theropods, which included the T-Rex and Velociraptor. This means every time you see a bird, you're looking at a distant relative of dinosaurs!

Outer Space Expansion

Explore the Universe!

Launch into 'Outer Space Expansion' and navigate through the cosmos with riddles and puzzles that reveal the universe's secrets. Learn about distant planets, stars, and the explorers who study them.

Each challenge propels your imagination into the vastness of space, where endless wonders await. Ready for a stellar adventure?

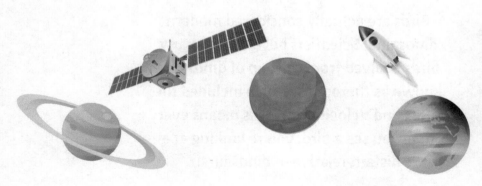

1. Misty and vast, I'm a stellar nursery in space, not just a cloud but a star-making place. What celestial wonder am I?

2. Adorned with rings and circled by moons, I'm a giant in the sky, not a jewel. Who am I in the solar parade?

3. I circle planets, catching eyes and light, not a moon or craft, shining bright at night. What am I, adorning the planets like jewels?

4. Tumbling through space, I roll on my side, a planetary oddity in the sun's ride. Which quirky planet am I?

JOKES

What kind of star wears sunglasses?
A movie star.

Why don't aliens eat clowns?
Because they taste funny.

Why did the robot volunteer for the space mission?
To upgrade its memory in zero-gravity!

What do you call a slow-moving spacecraft?
A space snail catching cosmic trails!

5. Known for my dusty red face and robotic visitors from place to place. I'm the fourth rock from our sun. What planet am I?

6. A cosmic outpost where humans reside, far above Earth where astronauts glide. What space home am I?

7. I'm the cosmic cradle of every sun, where stellar journeys first begun. What am I, a star in infancy?

8. f Earth was my cradle, Mars is my quest, roving the red to find science's best. Who am I, a wanderer of Martian plains?

What kind of lights did Noah use on the Ark?
Flood lights, but now astronauts use star lights!

Why didn't the astronaut land on the moon?
Because it was full!

What do you call an alien with three eyes?
An aliiien.

What did the astronaut cook for lunch?
An unidentifiable frying object.

9. Tail aglow when near the sun, through space I roam, never to run. What celestial wanderer am I?

10. A cosmic zone of rocky peers, orbiting between Martian and Jovian spheres. What am I, a celestial belt?

11. Zooming fast, I light the sky, a brief bright streak from up on high. What am I, a fleeting fire in the night?

12. Not Earth's sister by nature but size, a toxic beauty under solar rise. Who am I, veiled in acid and heat?

What do you call a lovestruck astronaut?
A space cadet in love.

Where do astronauts leave their spaceships?
At parking meteors.

Why did the planet go to the therapist?
Because it had too much space and felt empty.

Why do astronauts prefer using Linux?
Because they don't like Windows in space!

13. Visible without aid, I'm a distant world of methane shade. What icy giant am I, farthest seen with the naked eye?

14. I mark the months and pull the tides, Earth's loyal companion on celestial rides. What am I, a satellite natural and true?

15. Once a planet, now a dwarf, in the Kuiper Belt I hold my course. Who am I, downgraded but still in spin?

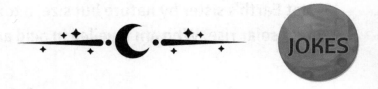

What game do astronauts like to play on the moon?
Crater tag.

Why did the astronaut break up with his girlfriend?
Because he needed space!

How do astronauts organize a party?
They planet!

What do you call a space explorer who sings really well?
An astro-noteworthy performer!

Brain Bender Boulevard

1. I am the ancient fire that lights the night sky, burning far longer than humans have lived. What am I?

2. I wear a dark cloak that covers mountains, valleys, and plains, but I am not cold. What am I?

3. I dance on the rings of Saturn but am not a dancer. What am I?

4. I hide my face by turning my back to you, no matter where you stand. What am I?

5. I am a watcher of the ages, my face marked by countless scribes. I never speak, yet I recount tales of battles and the quiet whispers of the wind. Light shines upon me, revealing stories of old. What am I?

Brain Bender Boulevard

6. I am the beginning of eternity and the end of time and space. I am essential to creation, and surround every place. What am I?

7. Ancient yet forever young, I am the keeper of history's greatest secrets. I am both light and darkness, holding the keys to the universe's extremes. What am I?

8. Silent and vast, I stretch beyond the limits of human sight. I cradle stars and planets but can swallow light. What am I?

9. My surface is scarred by my turbulent youth, yet I dance gracefully with many, though I am tied to only one. What am I?

10. Cloaked in invisibility, I hold the cosmos in my embrace. I guide the pathways of stars and galaxies yet leave no trace. My presence is inferred from the unseen forces I exert. What am I?

★Outer Space Expansion Answers

1. A nebula.
2. Saturn.
3. Rings of a planet.
4. Uranus.
5. Mars.
6. The International Space Station (ISS).
7. A protostar.
8. A rover.
9. A comet.
10. The asteroid belt.
11. A shooting star or meteor.
12. Venus.
13. Neptune.
14. The Moon.
15. Pluto.

Brain Bender Boulevard

1. A star.
2. The night sky.
3. Dust or ice particles in Saturn's rings.
4. The far side of the Moon.
5. The Moon. *whose craters have witnessed the history of the solar system.*
6. The letter 'E', found in the words space, time, and eternity.
7. A black hole.
8. The universe.
9. Jupiter.
10. The Dark matter.

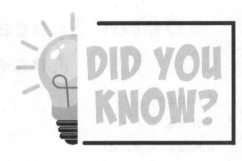

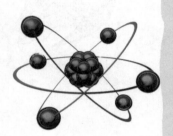

Dark Matter and Dark Energy

About 85% of the mass of the universe is dark matter, and dark energy makes up about 70% of the total energy. These components are invisible and detectable only through their gravitational effects and the way they influence the expansion of the universe.

Temperature of Space

The average temperature of outer space around the Earth is 2.7 Kelvin (-270.45 degrees Celsius, -454.81 degrees Fahrenheit), which is above absolute zero, the coldest temperature possible.

Space is completely silent because there is no atmosphere in space, which means there are no molecules for sound to travel through. This phenomenon is why astronauts use radios to communicate in space.

The largest volcano in our solar system is not on Earth, but on Mars. Olympus Mons is about 13.6 miles (22 kilometers) high, which makes it nearly three times the height of Mount Everest, and it spans about the size of the state of New Mexico.

There are more stars in the universe than grains of sand on all the Earth's beaches combined. Scientists estimate there could be about 100 billion galaxies in the universe, each with millions or even billions of stars.

Schoolyard Smiles

Laugh and Learn!

Welcome to 'Schoolyard Smiles,' where fun meets the classroom through a collection of school-themed riddles and jokes. Tackle clever puzzles and share giggles with friends as you explore subjects from math to history. Each challenge is designed to spark joy and curiosity, making learning an exciting adventure.
Get ready to solve, laugh, and learn!

1. Whirling tales without a whisper, where friendships form and giggles linger. What playground spinner am I?

2. I hold the hues of a magical palette, ready to sketch skies and rabbits. What vibrant box am I?

3. Every day I swing wide, letting dreams and adventures inside. What school gatekeeper am I?

4. We rustle with the breeze, whispering secrets beneath our leaves. What leafy listeners are we?

Why did the girl bring a ladder to school?
She wanted to reach new heights of learning!

What's the best place to grow flowers in school?
In the kinder-garden, where young plants meet young minds!

How do bees get to school?
They catch the school buzz!

Why did the clock in the cafeteria always run slow?
It always went back for seconds... and thirds!

RIDDLES

5. A field of dreams and competitive cheers, where players chase victories throughout the years. What am I?

6. With hands but no arms, I face you without eyes, counting your moments until the day dies. What keeper of time am I?

7. Voiceless, I sing a call that rings, to gather and guide with the joy it brings. What am I?

8. Stacked with tales and guarded by lore, where dragons soar and heroes roar. What treasure trove am I?

What's a snake's favorite subject?
Hiss-tory, especially the sss-sections on ancient times!

What do you call a geometry class after they learned about circles?
A round-table discussion!

Why was the equal sign so humble?
It knew it was never greater than or less than any other, only ever equal!

What school supply is always tired?
A knapsack, always taking a little nap between classes!

 **RIDDLES**

9. A mountain of nets and bars, where kids climb to reach the stars. What playground fixture am I?

10. Guardian of secrets and keeper of books, in my belly, you'll find snacks and hooks. What am I?

11. A slate of possibilities where lessons and imaginations race. What am I, a teacher's chalky space?

12. A path lined with memories and echoes of laughter, where lessons begin and friendships are captured. What am I?

 **JOKES**

What's the king of all school supplies?
The ruler, of course!

Why did the teacher wear sunglasses in class?
Because her students shone brighter than the sun!

How do you make sure your grades are always straight A's?
Line them up with a ruler!

Why do students always do their homework in the library?
Because that's where the best "plot" twists happen!

13. A world of numbers and shapes, where puzzles unravel and minds reshape. What book am I?

14. From here, adventurers and dreamers are led, a seat of wisdom where stories are fed. What am I, holding more than just a back?

15. I navigate through lessons and tales each day, a vessel of discovery where young minds play. What am I?

JOKES

Why did the science teacher head to the beach?
She needed to grade the sea!

Why did the geometry book seem so stressed?
Because all its problems were unsolved!

What should you do if a teacher rolls her eyes at you?
Catch them and ask for extra credit!

Why was the computer cold at school?
Because it left its Windows open!

Brain Bender Boulevard

1. Standing firm with arms wide, I encircle the laughter and secrets outside. Without moving, I watch over treasures: balls, jump ropes, and recess pleasures. What am I?

2. With no lips, I sing a sharp tune, calling players under the sun or moon. I command attention with my piercing cry, orchestrating games as time flies by. What am I?

3. Lined with lockers and bustling with feet, I'm a hallway where stories and students meet. Echoes of laughter, whispers, and calls fill me from the morning until the night falls. What am I?

4. Every morning, I start my voyage, steering through streets with a cargo most precious. With stops and starts, I carry dreams, traversing daily routes and streams. What am I?

5. In my chilly embrace, lunches wait—a guard of ice for food plates. From yogurts to sandwiches, apples to cakes, I keep them safe for midday breaks. What am I?

6. On my surface, continents sprawl, oceans twirl around an invisible ball. Hands spin tales of ancient lands, guiding young explorers with invisible hands. What am I?

7. My pages hold lines where thoughts are penned, secrets are kept, and stories extend. Each leaf a blank slate for daydreams and more, waiting for the pen's dance to explore. What am I?

8. In rows they stand, silent sentinels with keys, ready to awaken at the lightest breeze. Tap a button, start a program, create a world where art and numbers can jam. What am I?

9. Built with care, bolt by bolt, I rise—a playground knight. I challenge the brave with climbs and slides, a fortress of joy at every stride. What am I?

10. I stand in the corner, quiet and tall, catching secrets, jackets, and the occasional ball. A silent guardian of all your wares, from scarves in winter to the notes you share. What am I?

Schoolyard Smiles
Answers

1. A playground merry-go-round.
2. A box of crayons.
3. The schoolyard gate.
4. The trees in the schoolyard.
5. A soccer field.
6. The school clock.
7. The school bell.
8. The school library.
9. The school jungle gym.
10. A locker.
11. The classroom blackboard.
12. The school hallway.
13. A math workbook.
14. The teacher's chair.
15. The classroom.

Brain Bender Boulevard

1. A schoolyard fence.
2. A referee's whistle.
3. The school corridor.
4. A school bus.
5. The school cafeteria refrigerator.
6. A classroom globe.
7. A lined notebook.
8. A computer lab.
9. A playground structure.
10. A coat rack in the classroom.

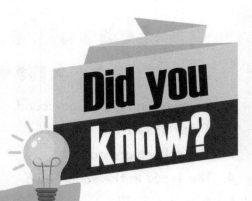

Did you know?

Oldest School in the World

Did you know that the world's oldest known school is the Shishi High School in Chengdu, China? It was founded way back in 141 BC as a place for learning and has been educating students for over two millennia!

Longest School Break

Children in Chile enjoy one of the longest summer breaks in the world, lasting from mid-December to early March. That's almost three months of vacation time!

The tradition of giving apples to teachers originated in the early 1700s in Denmark and Sweden. Farmers would pay their children's teachers with food because they could not afford monetary payment.

The world's first known calculator, the abacus, was used in schools for teaching mathematics hundreds of years ago. It is still used today in various parts of the world to help young children learn counting and arithmetic.

In South Korea, there is a holiday called 'Teacher's Day' where students show their appreciation by giving flowers and gifts to their teachers. This special day is celebrated annually on May 15th.

Wheels and Gears

Gear Up for Adventure!

Step into 'Wheels and Gears,' where every puzzle and joke is powered by motion and innovation. Discover the fascinating world of machines, from bicycles to cars and beyond. Solve riddles that crank up your brain and jokes that will have your gears turning with laughter.
It's time to rev up your imagination and explore the mechanics of fun!

1. I zip through tales on silent spokes, spinning adventures without any folks. What am I?

2. With hands that never greet and a face that never sees, I keep the time with endless ease. What am I?

3. By night I shine, leading the way, my beams cutting through shadows as I sway. What am I?

4. Small but mighty, I unlock your day with a turn and a click. What am I?

What do you call a bull that works in construction?
A bulldozer!

Why did the bicycle fall over?
Because it was two-tired to stand!

What did the shy traffic light say?
Don't look now, I'm changing colors!

What kind of car do eggs drive to breakfast?
A Yolkswagen Beetle!

5. Circles of comfort spun by my blades, I create breezes that never fade. What am I?

6. I chart courses and guide your ride, ensuring no destination can hide. What am I?

7. Perched up high, spinning silently above, I capture the still air of an attic with love. What am I?

8. Crank my handle to hear a tune, a crafted melody under the moon. What am I?

Why did the car pull over for a nap?
Because it had been driving in its dreams all night!

What do you call a party car that's out of fuel?
A Ford Siesta!

Why did the old car start a new career?
It wanted to switch gears and drive a new path!

9. Round and round where laughter's found, I carry children off the ground. What am I?

10. While you rest, I weave and spin, dreaming up worlds to let you in. What am I?

11. Swift and sleek, I glide on wheels, a street-surfing board of ollies and heels. What am I?

12. Inside a timepiece, I hide away, making minutes march every day. What am I?

What do you call a laughing motorcycle?
A Yamahahaha.

What's a car's favorite meal?
Brake-fast.

How do you stop a dog from barking in the back seat of a car?
Put him in the front seat!

Why do race cars have stripes?
So they don't get ticketed for speeding!

13. Morning ritual performed with beans, I turn them into a magical caffeine stream. What am I?

14. My wheels spin tales, my engine hums, taking you far from whence you come. What am I?

15. My reels spin tales of old and new, casting light on stories true. What am I?

What do you call a car that never stops joking?
A car-icature!

What part of a car is the laziest?
The wheels, because they are always tired!

Why are old race cars the best in history?
Because they have the best track records!

What kind of car does a Jedi drive?
A Toy-Yoda!

Brain Bender Boulevard

1. What has many teeth but can't bite, helps move a vehicle but isn't alive?

2. I silently guard the depths of your journey, capturing moments of truth and time without ever saying a word. What am I?

3. I stand still and watch every journey unfold, yet I travel far without moving an inch. I chart paths and destinations, a silent guide in the palm of your hand. What am I?

4. I embrace the road with every journey, feeling every twist and turn. Yet, I am bound and cannot wander off the path laid before me. What am I?

5. Invisible yet crucial, I fight against the rush of the wind, preserving order and control when speed tries to rule. What am I?

6. I am the unseen protector, springing to action only when disaster strikes. I embrace without arms and save without words. What am I?

7. Born from ancient sands, I transform under heat and pressure to carry you where feet cannot tread. I can show you the world, yet I can also be the end of the road. What am I?

8. I connect yet separate, engage yet disengage, all in the dance of gears and speed. What am I?

9. With hands that never applaud and numbers that never speak, I tell a tale of speed and time, ever watchful and never blind. What am I?

10. I twirl without dancing, pump without a heart, and come alive with the spark of a moment. What am I?

Wheels and Gears Answers

1. A bicycle in a book or story.
2. A clock.
3. A car's headlights.
4. A key.
5. A fan.
6. A GPS system in a vehicle.
7. A ceiling fan.
8. A music box.
9. A merry-go-round.
10. The subconscious mind.
11. A skateboard.
12. The gears in a clock.
13. A coffee grinder.
14. A car.
15. A film projector.

Brain Bender Boulevard

1. A gear.
2. A car's dashboard camera.
3. A GPS navigation system.
4. A car's tires.
5. Aerodynamics of a vehicle.
6. An airbag.
7. Glass, particularly a windshield.
8. A clutch in a manual transmission.
9. A car's speedometer or tachometer.
10. A car engine.

Wheels of History

The first known use of the wheel wasn't for transportation but for pottery. Around 3500 B.C., the Sumerians used wheels to create ceramics well before they thought to use them for chariots.

Gearing Up Through Time

The oldest known gears were found in the Antikythera mechanism, an ancient Greek astronomical device that dates back to around 100 BC. This complex machine used gears to predict lunar and solar eclipses.

Revolution on Two Wheels

The modern bicycle's gear system was not introduced until the late 19th century, revolutionizing how bikes were ridden and making cycling much easier and more efficient for longer distances.

The world's first traffic light was installed in London in 1868 near the Houses of Parliament to control the flow of horse carriages. However, it exploded less than a month after it was implemented due to a gas leak!

The fastest speed ever recorded on a bicycle was 183.93 miles per hour by Denise Mueller-Korenek in 2018. She rode her specially designed bike across the Bonneville Salt Flats in Utah, setting a new world record.

In the Netherlands, there are more bicycles than people. The country is known for its extensive and well-used bike paths, with about 17 million bicycles for 17 million residents, making cycling a major mode of transportation.

Create Your Own Riddles!

Hey there, young riddler!
Ready to create your very own brain-teasing riddles? Follow these simple steps, and soon you'll be making everyone scratch their heads trying to solve your clever riddles!

Instructions:

1. **Choose Your Answer First:** Think of something fun or interesting you want your friends to guess. It could be an object, an animal, or anything else you like!

2. **Think About What It Does:** What special things can your answer do? Does it make a sound, move in a unique way, or is it used for something specific?

3. **Use Your Imagination:** Think of fun ways to describe your answer without giving it away. Use comparisons or describe what it feels like, looks like, sounds like, or even smells like!

4. **Keep It Simple:** Try to describe your answer in one or two sentences. The best riddles are both tricky and easy to remember.

5. **Test It Out:** Tell your riddle to family or friends without telling them the answer. See if they can guess it. If it's too hard or too easy, you might want to change a few words.

Loading . . .

Example Riddles:
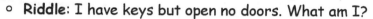

- **Example 1:**
  - ○ **Riddle:** I have keys but open no doors. What am I?
  - ○ **Answer:** A piano.

- **Example 2:**
  - ○ **Riddle:** I'm tall when I'm young and short when I'm old. What am I?
  - ○ **Answer:** A candle.

- **Example 3:**
  - ○ **Riddle:** What has a ring but no finger?
  - ○ **Answer:** A telephone.

- **Example 4:**
  - ○ **Riddle:** I run all around the playground but never move. What am I?
  - ○ **Answer:** A fence.

Activity Prompt: Now it's your turn! Try to create a riddle about your favorite animal or your favorite toy. Remember, the fun is in the guessing, so make it tricky!

Closing Encouragement: Creating riddles is not just fun; it's a great way to use your imagination and test your word skills. Keep practicing, and you'll be a riddle master in no time.

Happy riddling!

  NOTES

_____

_____

_____

_____

_____

_____

_____

_____

_____

_____

_____

_____

_____

_____

_____

_____

_____

_____

NOTES

  NOTES

NOTES

ABOUT THE AUTHOR

Hello Adventurers!
I'm Christiana, and my world is a canvas painted with words and wonder. My journey started in graphic design, but I found my true magic in creating moments that make our hearts sing.

When I'm not spinning tales or crafting unique experiences, I'm in my creative nook, inspired by the breathtaking landscapes of Scotland. Whether it's painting scenes that capture the imagination, making candles that tell stories, or transforming spaces with whimsical decorations, I'm all about bringing dreams to life.

But the fun doesn't stop there! My passion for storytelling has blossomed into these activity books, where every page is a new adventure. Packed with stories, puzzles, and a dash of magic, they're designed to spark curiosity and inspire learning.

Ready for more adventures? Let's journey together through a world where creativity knows no bounds!

Thank you for joining me on this delightful journey. Here's to many more stories, laughs, and learning moments!

OTHER BOOKS BY THE AUTHOR

Second Grade Jokes and Riddles

Want to keep your second grader laughing while sharpening their brainpower?

Spark laughter and boost **critical thinking** with this playful collection of **jokes and riddles** designed for **second-graders**.

Christiana Berg combines **humor** and **brain-teasing fun** to make learning an adventure.

Featuring **brainy riddles, hilarious jokes**, and a **Creative Corner** for kids to invent their own jokes, this book is perfect for enhancing problem-solving skills and encouraging creativity.

Dive into endless laughter and learning—ideal for kids who love to laugh and think outside the box!

Scan Me

Kids Kaleidoscope: A Journey of Fun and Learning 5+

Unlock the magic of learning with activities that blend fun and education! Perfect for kids aged 5 and up, **"Kids Kaleidoscope: A Journey of Fun and Learning 5+"**, offers a vibrant mix of coloring pages, literacy activities, math exercises, and puzzles.

Each page is designed to spark creativity, strengthen skills, and ignite curiosity.

- Colorful adventures and puzzles to boost problem-solving skills.
- Engaging stories and writing exercises to enhance literacy.
- Fun math challenges to build a strong foundational understanding.

Let your child's learning journey begin with a splash of fun!

Scan Me

Magic In The Pine Mountain: An Awesome Journey Tale

Dive into a world of adventure with "**Magic In The Pine Mountain**," where every page is an adventure and every moment a lesson in courage, friendship, and teamwork.

Designed for young readers, including those with dyslexia, this story unfolds in the mystical Whispering Pines Mountain. Join Willow, Alex, Lily, Oliver, and Max as they embark on a quest to restore the rainbow's missing colors.

Features:
- Dyslexia-Friendly Design: Large print and clear spacing make the magical journey accessible and enjoyable.
- Vibrant Illustrations: Full-page artwork that immerses you in a visually stunning, magical world.
- Timeless Lessons: Discover stories of bravery, the power of friendship, and the importance of teamwork.

Perfect for any young reader who loves fantasy and adventure. Start your journey today!

Made in United States
Troutdale, OR
12/12/2024

26328559R00066